Contents

Yánnina: A Changing Town

Yánnina is the capital of the Epirus region of north-western Greece. It lies on the shores of Lake Pamvótis surrounded by the high mountains of the Pindus range. Due to its location, Yánnina and its nearby towns and villages were quite isolated until after the mid-twentieth century. In the 1950s and 1960s thousands of people abandoned Yánnina and migrated abroad or to the capital, Athens. Since then there have been great improvements in the region's road network, connecting Yánnina with Athens and other Greek cities.

Although agriculture has steadily declined in the region, the city is still famous for its yoghurt, cheese and other dairy products while intensive poultry-rearing has become an important new industry in the countryside nearby. Yánnina is also renowned for its tradition of metal working and jewellery making. Greek and foreign tourists are attracted to Yánnina and they visit the city for its rich cultural history and, nearby, some of the most spectacular scenery in Greece.

Yánnina has one of Greece's largest universities, which has greatly increased the number of young people living in the city. Since 1971 the city's population has increased by over a third. It is continuing to grow as more housing, new public buildings, hotels and other facilities are constructed. Although since the 1950s Yánnina has lost much of its traditional architecture, it still preserves a bustling old quarter with narrow streets, and stone houses with wooden balconies. Yánnina has transformed from a remote, market town into a modern and vibrant city with a fascinating mix of old and new, of traditional and modern.

▲ The Aslan Pasha Mosque within Yánnina's ancient fortress was built in 1618.

▼ A modern luxury hotel near Lake Pamvótis built in the architectural style of a traditional local mansion.

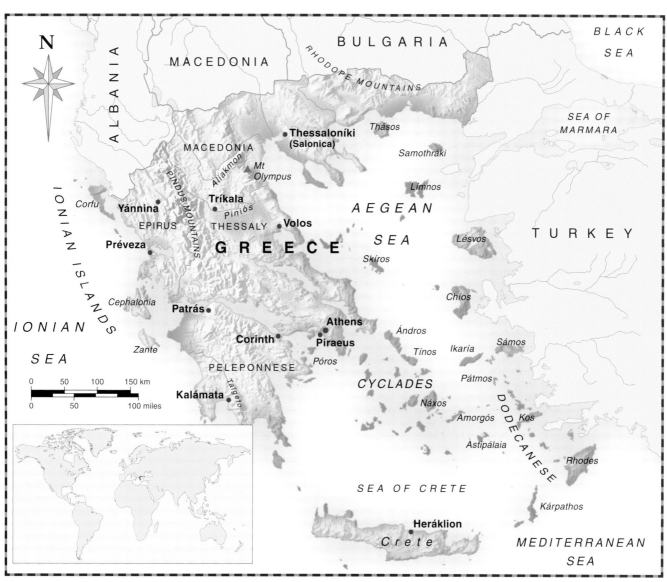

▲ *This map shows the main geographical features of Greece, as well as places mentioned in this book.*

GREECE: KEY FACTS

Area: 131,957 square km
Population: 10,939,771 (2001 census)
Population density: 83 people per square km
Capital city: Athens
Other main cities: Thessaloníki (Salonika); Piraeus; Patras
Highest mountain: Mount Olympus (2,904 m)
Longest river: Aliakmon (297 km)
Main language: Modern Greek
Main religions: Greek Orthodoxy (98 per cent), Muslim (1.5 per cent)
Currency: Euro

2 Past Times

The heritage of ancient Greece

The history of Greece spans over 5,000 years. Ancient Greek culture and civilization, which flourished around the shores of the Mediterranean, reached its peak around 500 BC, producing some of the world's greatest artists, dramatists, politicians, philosophers, mathematicians, doctors and scientists. In the second century BC, Greece fell to the Romans. When, in AD 330, the Roman Empire was split in two, the eastern Greek-speaking part formed the Byzantine Empire. From the eleventh century, a succession of foreign peoples invaded Greece, and by the late 1500s it had been absorbed into the Ottoman Empire.

The beginnings of Modern Greece

Greece was dominated by Ottoman Turkish rule for nearly 400 years. In 1821 the Greeks rose up against their Turkish rulers, winning their independence in 1830. However it was a much smaller country than it is today, for much of Greece did not gain independence until the late 1800s or during the Balkan Wars of 1912-13.

▲ The Acropolis, built in the 5th century BC, presides over the skyline of modern Athens.

◄ The Greek Parliament building overlooks Syntagma Square. In the foreground is the National Guard, the Évzones, in Greek national dress.

During World War II Greece was occupied by the Germans. Following its liberation in 1945, the country was plunged almost immediately into a civil war (1946-49) in which the government defeated the Communist Left, bringing Greece into line with the West. In 1952 Greece joined NATO.

Post-1960s

In 1967 a group of military colonels overthrew the government in a *coup d'état*. Their military dictatorship lasted until 1974 when a student revolution began its downfall. Meanwhile the monarchy had gone into exile, and in a referendum that followed the return of democracy, the Greek people voted against restoration of the monarchy. Since then Greece has been a parliamentary democracy with an elected parliament led by a president. In 1981 Greece joined the European Union (EU). In 2002, the Euro replaced the Greek drachma, the oldest currency in the world.

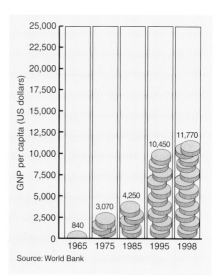

Source: World Bank

▲ *The money Greece earns from goods and services it produces has increased dramatically since 1965.*

IN THEIR OWN WORDS

'My name is Élena Nazíri. I live in Trikala in the plain of Thessaly. Trikala was in Turkish hands for hundreds of years. Nazir isn't a Greek name, it's Turkish. My great-grandfather took a Turkish name but he also fought in the resistance against the Turks. This part of Greece wasn't liberated until 1881.

'Life for people today is changing so rapidly. When my father was growing up, they had no electricity at home. He had a good education though. Now people have air conditioning in their homes and lots of other luxuries. Everyone has cars. It's easy to travel from one place to another. Greece is like one big village now.'

3

Landscape and Climate

Greece is Europe's southernmost country. Situated at the end of the Balkan landmass, mainland Greece forms a peninsula jutting out into the Mediterranean Sea. Greece is also an archipelago of some 2,000 islands, although only 170 of them are inhabited. It is a country of very varied landscape and climate. Tourist postcards usually depict its sandy beaches, blue seas and hot sunshine, but in fact three-quarters of Greece is mountainous country, and its winters can be very cold and wet.

▲ Land rising up steeply from the sea is typical of much of the Greek coastline.

Mountains

The Pindus Mountains, running north to south, form the backbone of mainland Greece. In the north-east, creating the border with Bulgaria, are the wooded Rhodope Mountains. Other mountains include the Taygetus in the Peloponnese, and the White Mountains of Crete.

Greece's mountains form many steep cliffs and deep, narrow gorges with rivers below. Their slopes may be forested with beech, oak, chestnut and pine, or covered with dense, thorny scrub. Elsewhere, as in the Mani region of the Peloponnese, the limestone slopes are dry, rocky and barren, resembling stony deserts.

▼ A hillside village in the Epirus. In early May the lower slopes provide rich pasture land while the peaks above often still have snow.

IN THEIR OWN WORDS

'My name is Grigoris Kitsoulis. I'm 82 years old. I have lived all my life in this village, Polystafyllo, in the Epirus. When I was young I used to go hunting in the woods for rabbits and birds. These were luxury foods for our family. Many people around here used to hunt. They hunted wild boar, wolves, foxes and rabbits. There aren't many animals in the woods today. In 20 years' time, this will be an abandoned place. The houses will only be used as holiday homes. Nobody will take care of the landscape and the wilderness will return.

'The climate is changing, too. We used to have much more snow in the past. It doesn't seem to snow so often here, and it rains a lot less, too. It often used to rain for 10 to 20 days at a time. That's rare today.'

Lowlands

Most of Greece's lowlands stretch along its coastal areas. The main inland lowlands are the plains of Thessaly in central Greece, Macedonia in the north and Thrace in the north-east. Fertile lowlands are also found in the Peloponnese.

Islands

The landscape of the Greek islands is very varied. The Ionian Islands off the west coast of Greece, which include Corfu and Cephalonia, are green and comparatively lush due to heavy winter rainfall. In contrast, the Cyclades islands in the Aegean Sea are rocky, dry and wind-swept. Crete combines high arid peaks with lower green slopes and fertile plains.

▼ *A view across the Gulf of Corinth to mainland Greece. In the foreground are olive trees and tall, dark cypresses, which are typical of the Greek landscape.*

Climate

The summers in Greece are generally hot and dry, and the winters mild and wet. However, temperature and rainfall patterns vary considerably between island groups, and between coastal and mountainous regions. In winter, the average January temperature in Thessaloníki is around 6 °C, although it can drop as low as –4 °C. In Athens it averages 10 °C. Summer temperatures tend to vary less, averaging 28 °C in July but often reaching highs of 40 °C. In northern and mountainous regions the winter often brings heavy snowfalls, and on a winter's day Crete's high peaks may have snow on them although the sea below is warm enough for swimming.

▲ Farmers irrigating their crops in the plains of central Greece.

Forest fires

Greece's hot, dry summer months bring the threat of forest fires. Following devastating fires in 1998, the number of firemen, fire stations and amount of fire-fighting equipment available in high-risk areas was vastly increased. The authorities run seminars for people living near forests explaining how to combat the danger of fire. Every summer, posters, billboards and announcements on television warn against the risk of fires. As a result, since the late 1990s, the loss of forest land and vegetation to fire has dropped dramatically.

▶ A mountain pass winds through conifer woods in central Greece.

Earthquakes

Greece lies on more than one fault line in the earth's crust and mild tremors are not uncommon. One fault line runs from north to south along the west coast of Greece and down to the Peloponnese. In 1986 Kalamata and some surrounding villages were devastated by an earthquake that left over 12,000 people homeless. Many buildings, poorly constructed in the 1960s, were destroyed. In 1999 Athens was hit by an earthquake that made thousands homeless but fortunately caused few deaths. The Greek army is well trained to act swiftly in providing emergency shelter, water and relief supplies.

▶ *Looking at this peaceful scene it is hard to imagine that parts of Greece lie on fault lines and have experienced damaging earthquakes.*

IN THEIR OWN WORDS

'I'm Grigoris Mihos. I'm 13 years old and I live in a village near the town of Préveza, on the west coast of Greece. There are very high mountains all around us. Look, even now in May, you can see snow on them. Our water comes from the mountains. It rains a lot here so we rarely have problems with water shortages, but I know it's a problem for many villages, especially if there are factories or industries in the area that use a lot of water. We're lucky. In summer it gets very hot here, and the mosquitoes are a great nuisance, especially around the marshy lands a little further south.'

4

Natural Resources

Energy sources

Most of Greece's electricity is generated by power stations fuelled by lignite (poor quality brown coal), which is mined from the Pindus Mountains. Greece's energy needs have been increasing steadily but burning lignite, although cheap, is highly polluting. As a result, the government has banned the construction of new lignite power stations while it hopes to increase the number of gas-fired stations. Approximately 10 per cent of Greece's energy is generated by hydro-electricity.

Greece has vast renewable energy sources in the form of sunlight, wind and wave power, but there has been slow progress in developing these resources. Solar panels on rooftops are widely used to heat hot water, but solar power stations are extremely expensive to build and to date none have been built. There are wind farms on Crete, Naxos and other Aegean Islands, and the next decade is likely to see the construction of many more.

▲ *Solar panels and television aerials on a typical roof of a modern Greek house.*

◄ *A modern oil refinery on the outskirts of Corinth, in the north-east of the Peloponnese.*

Agriculture

Although less than 30 per cent of Greece is arable land, historically the Greek economy was based on agriculture. Rural people lived by subsistence farming, relying on their flocks of sheep and goats for milk, cheese, yoghurt and meat, their vineyards and olive trees for wine and olive oil. In the last few decades subsistence farming has declined rapidly. However, farmers have increased their agricultural output as subsidies from the EU have helped to modernize their farming practices. Principal products are olive oil, olives, citrus fruit, corn, wheat, cotton, rice and grapes. In recent decades the number of factory-farmed pigs and chickens has increased. In the case of tobacco, however, the EU has subsidized a decrease in its production to restrict the consumption of cigarettes, which grew by 6 per cent in the 1990s.

▲ *Market gardeners use plastic tunnels to extend the growing season of vegetables and other crops.*

IN THEIR OWN WORDS

'My full name is Evángelos Grigoríou, but Evángelos is commonly shortened to Lakis. I'm a farmer. Agriculture is not an easy way of life in a country as rocky as this. Fortunately we get plenty of rain here. We used to have many more animals, including cows, horses and donkeys. You don't see a lot of cows in Greece because they need better pasture land than sheep and goats. We still have goats so we have our own milk from which to make cheese and yoghurt.

'Until the 1950s there were few tractors around here. People used donkeys to transport their crops and firewood. They rode their donkeys too. Since the 1970s all the local farmers use tractors. They've made their fields bigger, too. If I were twenty years old now, I'd choose to study first and then come back here to farm as a better farmer.'

Fishing

Greeks have lived off fish from their seas for thousands of years. In the past the population of many Greek islands depended almost exclusively on fishing for a living. Greek fish markets usually display a wide diversity of fish, ranging from small whitebait and sardines to large fish such as swordfish, grouper and tuna. Local seafood also includes lobsters, sea urchins, octopus, cuttlefish, squid and mussels. However, overfishing and water pollution have reduced fish stocks. The government is trying to improve the situation by regulating the number of commercial fishing licences and introducing fishing quotas. Restrictions have also been introduced relating to fishing methods and against catching fish that are too small and young to breed. Meanwhile local supply cannot satisfy demand, especially during the tourist season. As a result, Greece now imports a wide range of fresh and frozen fish from Israel and the Far East, and mackerel and cod from the North Sea. With the exception of farmed fish (see page 41), exports tend to be limited to large tuna which is exported to Japan and the Far East.

▲ A colourful array of native fish (sea bream, sea bass and octopus) and imported salmon in a fish market.

▼ A busy harbour scene with small fishing boats. Greeks often buy fresh seafood direct from fishermen at the harbourside.

IN THEIR OWN WORDS

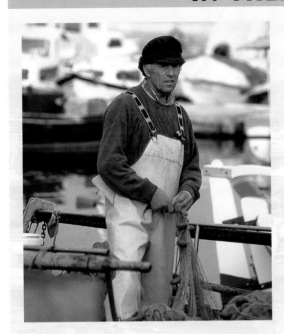

'My name is Dimítris Páppas. I have been going fishing since my uncle used to take me as a small boy. His caique didn't have an engine as most boats have now. In the evening we would row out to sea to drop the nets. Then we would go out again in the very early hours to collect them. Fish has always been a staple part of the modern Greek diet just as it was for the ancient Greeks. Greater awareness of the benefits of eating more fish, and recent scares about possible diseases associated with meat, have made a lot of people want to eat more fish. But things are getting harder because there are far fewer fish out there. I sell my catch locally – to the restaurants around here, and in the town market.'

Minerals

Greece is rich in a variety of minerals. It has large reserves of bauxite, which is used to make aluminium, and it produces some 36 per cent of the EU's natural magnesite (used in medicines, fertilizers and in industry). Greece also mines zinc (used with copper to make brass, and to galvanize steel), iron ore (for iron and steel) and lead. Marble has been quarried in Greece since ancient times and it is still widely used today. The manufacturing of cement, which is produced from limestone, is a primary industry. Greece is second to China in world production of cement.

▲ *Limestone quarries such as this one are found all over Greece.*

5 The Changing Environment

Urbanization

In the last fifty years Greece has experienced urbanization on a huge scale. Post-war industrial growth around Athens caused the population to soar as people came to the city looking for work and a better life. Since World War II it has transformed from a city of about 700,000 into an urban sprawl of nearly 4 million people.

The very swift pace in the growth of Athens resulted in poor city planning. Most people live in flats in concrete apartment blocks that have balconies but no gardens. Below the streets are noisy, congested and full of traffic. The shortages in housing are a huge problem. The city has very few green or open spaces. Meanwhile new buildings are continuously encroaching on the countryside around Athens and Piraeus. However, most people who work in Athens want to live within the city as its transport system does not allow for quick and easy commuting to work.

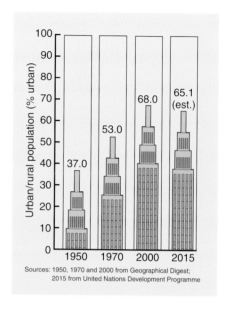

Sources: 1950, 1970 and 2000 from Geographical Digest; 2015 from United Nations Development Programme

▲ The number of people living in urban areas has increased dramatically in the last 50 years.

◄ An ancient archaeological site against a background of new building work in the heart of Athens.

Athens and air pollution

Athens lies in a plain surrounded by hills on three sides. This contributes greatly to its pollution problems as traffic fumes and industrial smog are trapped above the city. During very hot weather, the city's pollution can cause health and respiratory problems, especially among the elderly and infirm. Acid rain has also caused damage to the stonework of the city's ancient monuments.

The city's authorities now monitor pollution levels in order to predict and avert pollution crises. Traffic reduction measures include restricting drivers to use of their cars on alternate days according to their car number plates, and diverting traffic away from congested areas. More recently, there has been huge investment in Athens' transportation system – which includes a metro – and pedestrianization of many inner city areas.

▲ *Athens' yellow trolleybuses complement the city's extensive network of buses.*

IN THEIR OWN WORDS

'My name is Maria Kóllia. I come from the north of Greece, from a mountain village near Kozáni, in Macedonia. I am a teacher of English in a foreign-language school. I came to live in Athens because of the better work prospects here. But Athens is not an easy place to live in and it continues to get harder. The city is overcrowded. Athens' biggest problem is the traffic. People's health is suffering.

'I feel the government is not doing enough to help the overpopulation problem of Greece's cities. I fear that they will continue to grow. Public money should be distributed more evenly throughout the different regions of the country. This would help limit migration towards the cities. Fortunately village life has become much better due to improvements in living conditions, as well as in transport and communication. Some young people now are choosing to remain in the country. I will return there when I retire.'

Water pollution

As elsewhere in the Mediterranean, sea pollution is a problem in Greek waters. In the early days following Greece's industrialization, the sea around urban centres served as a dumping ground for sewage and industrial waste. Increases in the use of fertilizers and pesticides in farming also contributed to river and sea water pollution.

However, great improvements have been made in waste management and a reduction in the use of harmful chemicals near sources of drinking water. Today, over ninety per cent of Greece's coastal waters are fit for bathing.

▲ *Water pollution is a problem in Greece. However, in recent years this has greatly improved.*

Water shortages

Water shortages have always been a problem in Greece, especially in areas that have to rely on water being 'imported' by shipping tankers. Households commonly use cisterns or underground tanks to store rainwater which is collected from the roofs. Alongside tourism, farming and agriculture are placing a huge pressure on Greece's water supplies.

Many Greek farmers pump water up from boreholes that draw from the water table.

▶ *A river bed in late spring. In mountainous areas they can rapidly fill with water during times of heavy rainfall.*

IN THEIR OWN WORDS

'I am Níkos Agelídis. I am 16 years old and live with my family in Athens. It's a very noisy city. As well as all the cars, taxis and buses, lots of people use motorbikes and motorcycles to weave in and out of the traffic. The motorcycles are very noisy. It's hardly ever quiet in the centre of Athens. The authorities should do a lot more to limit noise levels.

'At school we are taught about the environment for about one hour every week. Even so, we are not as aware of the environment as I think we should be. It's not good to see rubbish lying around in the city. Police should be given more power to fine people who drop litter and who make unnecessary noise.'

The government is trying to persuade farmers to grow crops that do not need heavy irrigation. Meanwhile households and businesses that have high water consumption levels have had to deal with water rationing and increased water charges.

Noise pollution

In many of Greece's major cities, the number of people living in a relatively small area has created problems with noise pollution. The combined effect of car horns, motorbikes, traffic and air conditioning units creates a level of noise that can be stressful to live with. The long working day and socializing until late into the night mean that there are very few hours of calm. The quietest hours of the day are during the mid-afternoon siesta when many shops close and people return home for an afternoon rest.

▶ *Pedestrian and traffic congestion in Athens. It is seldom quiet in the city.*

Tourism

Greece is one of the world's most popular holiday destinations with over twelve million foreign visitors each year. Inevitably this has had an enormous impact on Greece's landscape and environment, and places great pressures on the country's infrastructure, including its water supplies, waste disposal, road building and agriculture. Huge areas of Greece's island coastlines have been developed to appeal to tourists, with hotels, swimming pools, restaurants and bars. On some islands, many local people have given up their self-sufficient way of life, and even their land, in favour of building and owning a hotel, a bar or souvenir shop. Olive groves and vineyards are no longer tended as people buy produce rather than grow their own. Traditional stone houses have been abandoned or knocked down to build new concrete houses and apartment blocks. A disregard for building regulations means that there has been very little control of how and where construction has taken place although, increasingly, the authorities are taking steps to control new building

▲ *Ferries carry tourists to the many beautiful Greek islands.*

◄ *Construction work on road tunnels under the Pindus mountains. The tunnels will form part of the Egnatía Odós, a major highway that will link the international port of Igoumenitsa with the central and eastern side of Greece.*

In recent years the Greek tourist industry has been looking at ways to appeal to visitors, attracted by high standards of accommodation and good facilities. It would like to see fewer package holiday-makers who typically do not have much money to spend. Nationally, the Greek government is supporting the construction of more harbours and yacht marinas so as to promote Greece as a cruising and sailing destination. Locally, a growing number of tourist enterprises are promoting eco-tourism and special interest holidays centred around, for example, bird watching in northern Greece, mountain trekking in the Epirus, or wild flower spotting in Crete. Such developments mean a spreading of tourism to areas of Greece other than its coast and archaeological sites, as well as a longer tourist season.

▲ *A group of tourists shelter from the sun during a guided tour of the ancient site of Olympia.*

IN THEIR OWN WORDS

'My name is Voúla Theodoráki. I work as a tour guide here on the island of Póros, off the coast of the Peloponnese. Tourism on the island really took off in the 1970s, and by the early 1980s it was booming. Ninety per cent of the island's economy is dependent on it. The increase in tourism does put the island under pressure though. Sometimes, in the height of the tourist season when the island is full, the local water supply doesn't meet the demand. Water has to be brought from the mainland. Occasionally we have problems with the power supply too. Litter can be a problem. Fortunately we have many more litter bins than we used to, as well as more road sweepers and dust carts.'

Wildlife conservation

The Greeks have always been passionate about hunting, from large animals such as wild boar down to the smallest birds. The country's once rich wildlife has been greatly depleted although the mountains are still home to wild boar, bears, wolves and wild cats, as well as some rare raptors. Today Greece has a substantial number of national parks. As is often the case, however, conservation initiatives are not always welcomed by everyone. For instance, some Greek fishermen used to hunt the Mediterranean monk seal because they saw them as a threat to local fish stocks. A marine reserve in the northern Sporades now protects this endangered seal. On Zante, tourists are urged to keep away from the sandy beaches where the loggerhead sea turtle comes ashore to nest, but similarly some locals see such moves as harmful to their tourist businesses.

Greece has a diversity of wetlands, including river deltas, salt marshes and lagoons. These areas are remarkably rich in flora and fauna, and provide nesting and breeding ground for water birds, including ducks, herons and a rare species of pelican. A number of bird sanctuaries has been set up in an effort to preserve their populations.

▲ *Tortoises are a common sight in the wild.*

◀ *A sign promoting awareness of the importance of trees and the environment.*

A greener future?

Greece has lagged far behind most of Europe in confronting its environmental problems. However public awareness of green issues is growing as more and more people take an interest in the state of the environment. Helped by EU funding, the government has put substantial investment into promoting more environmentally-sound practices as it improves the country's services and infrastructure. Meanwhile, tourism interests have helped to add impetus to the conservation movement and the protection of places of outstanding natural beauty or of particular historical and architectural interest.

▶ *In provincial towns recycling facilities are often limited to waste paper only.*

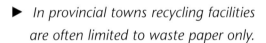

IN THEIR OWN WORDS

'My name is Katerína Míta. This is my friend Anna Geládi. I am 15 and she's 13. We live in a residential neighbourhood of Athens. Litter isn't a serious problem around here but it is in other parts of the city. I think people don't think about recycling their rubbish because there are very few recycling facilities, limited to certain areas. Our parents pay a local tax to cover such services but I think the government doesn't do enough to provide facilities. There is so much more rubbish now than there was in the past. A lot of it has to do with all the packaging around food.'

6

The Changing Population

Population growth

In the 1950s and 60s, some 10 per cent of Greece's population emigrated. The annual birth rate then was around 20 per 1,000 people. Today it stands at less than 10 per 1,000. Despite these factors, Greece's population has grown from close to 8 million in the late 1950s to nearly 11 million today. The population growth is largely due to a massive influx of economic migrants, primarily from neighbouring Albania, but

▲ *A busy street in central Athens.*

also from eastern Europe, the Middle East and Asia. Today Greece's immigrant population is close to 10 per cent of the population, and makes up a high percentage of the country's unskilled labour force.

Population distribution

As recently as the 1960s, well over half of Greece's population lived in rural areas. Today over 66 per cent live in urban areas, with 40 per cent alone in Athens. A further 15 per cent of Greeks live in Thessaloniki. Corfu and Crete are two of the most densely populated islands.

Living longer

Greece has one of the world's largest populations of the elderly. The proportion of elderly people in Greece in the late 1990s was estimated to be 23 per cent. This is expected to rise to 28 per cent by 2020. Greek women typically outlive men by five to six years.

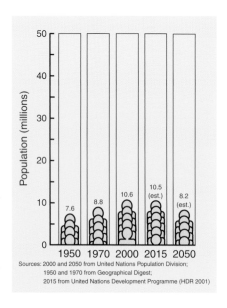

Sources: 2000 and 2050 from United Nations Population Division;
1950 and 1970 from Geographical Digest;
2015 from United Nations Development Programme (HDR 2001)

▲ *This graph shows how population growth in Greece is predicted to decline.*

IN THEIR OWN WORDS

'My name is Maria Lavránou. My sister and I grew up in Athens but both my parents are originally from Corfu. My mother was only 17 when she got married to get away from village life and move to Athens. She had both my sister and me before she was twenty. My grandmother came to live with us here so both my parents could go out to work.

'My life is very different from my mother's. I am 26 years old now. I am a flautist studying for my Master's Degree at the Athens Conservatoire. I've nearly finished my studies. I'd like to spend the next five years in a steady job, teaching or playing in an orchestra, then settle down to have a family. This is typical of most middle-class families. In the country, people get married a little younger. I still live at home. I don't have enough money to leave home and pay for my studies. It's quite usual for children to stay with their parents until they're about 28 or even 32. My parents and grandparents ask me from time to time when I'm going to marry but they aren't pressurizing me. They understand that my career is more important. I'd like to have two or three children but unemployment and the cost of university education have to be considered.'

Ageing parents generally live with one of their children. Care of the elderly usually falls on a daughter or a daughter-in-law. Until recently, Greece had relatively few retirement and nursing homes. This will have to change in the future as the elderly increasingly outnumber the young.

► *An elderly couple with their grandchild. Life expectancy in Greece is one of the highest in the world.*

Greece's minority populations

Ethnic Greeks form 98 per cent of the country's population. The other 2 per cent is made up of Turks, Sarakatsans, Vlachs and Roma, or gypsies. Most of Greece's Muslim population is concentrated in western Thrace, while the Epirus and Macedonia are home to most Sarakatsans and Vlachs. Traditionally both the Sarakatsans and the Vlachs were nomadic shepherds, who moved between the mountains and plains according to where they would find pasture for their sheep and goats. Unlike the Sarakatsans who speak a form of Greek, the language of the Vlachs is closer to Latin.

Greece's gypsy population is concentrated on the mainland with large numbers now living around Athens' suburbs. After the Albanians, Roma gypsies form the largest ethnic minority in Greece. Some have settled lifestyles but about half live in tented encampments where they may seek unskilled work or make a living by selling baskets, plastic furniture or rugs.

In past times Greece was home to one of the oldest established Jewish communities. Its Jewish population was spread throughout most of Greece's mainland towns, with a very large number concentrated in Thessaloníki especially, and on many of its islands as well. During the German occupation of Greece in World War II, the Greek Jewish community suffered great losses. Thousands were transported to Nazi camps in eastern Europe. Today there are still Jewish communities in Thessaloníki, Yánnina and Vólos, with the largest number of Jews living in Athens.

▲ *Gypsy women typically dress in bright-coloured, patterned clothes and full skirts.*

The Greek diaspora

Greece has a long history of emigration. In the 1950s and 1960s, thousands of people from all parts of the country, many for political as well as economic reasons, went to live and work in Germany, Australia, America or Canada. The large Greek communities they formed in foreign cities are known as the Greek diaspora. Hardly a Greek village exists that has not been affected by emigration. On the other hand, many communities have benefited greatly from money made abroad that has been brought or sent back to Greece. Today, apart from large numbers of students going abroad to attend foreign universities, Greece's rate of emigration is low.

▲ *A Greek woman working in a bakery in Mexico. Her family is one of many that emigrated from Greece.*

IN THEIR OWN WORDS

'I am Dashamir Bali. I am Albanian but I left my home in Tirana, the capital of Albania, in 1993 to come to Greece. I had worked for four years there in the police force. We have great economic problems in our country. I didn't want to leave but life there was very difficult. I was in my early twenties when I left my mother, father and brother to come here to find work. I haven't had any problems settling in Greece. At the moment I am working as a waiter. It's hard work, especially at holiday times and during the summer when the island becomes very busy. I try to go back to Tirana every two months to see my family and my girlfriend. I drive back. It's a long way by car and it takes many, many hours. I hope that when I have kids, they will be able to have a good life in Albania.'

7

Changes at Home

Family life

Family life is important to most Greeks and has a powerful influence on how they live. The traditional Greek household consists of an extended family of several generations living under one roof. This is still true today, although different groups within the extended family may live in separate flats within the same apartment block. Family members feel a strong sense of responsibility for each other, and depend on one another for emotional, social and often, economic support.

▼ *An extended family gathering share a meal on Easter Monday. All over Greece, families come together for religious holidays.*

In the past there was considerable pressure, particularly on girls, if, by their late twenties, they had not married or at least become engaged to be married. After marriage, the bride would generally be expected to live with her husband's family. Today couples are choosing to marry later than in the past. They have greater social freedom and may choose to live away from the family home.

In the past, Greek women were expected to provide their husband with a dowry upon marriage. The dowry was usually a combination of money, linen and household goods, farmland or a building plot. The dowry system was abolished by law in 1983, although it still lingers on, especially in rural areas. Another significant change for women has been that, unlike in the past, upon marriage they now retain the property deeds in their own name.

The legalization of civil marriages in 1982, and simplification of the divorce process has changed the way marriage is viewed in Greece. In the past divorce was relatively uncommon and widely disapproved of by both the public and the Church. In recent years divorce rates have risen dramatically as has the number of single-parent families.

▶ *This young Greek couple are likely to marry later than their parents' generation, and are less likely to stay married.*

IN THEIR OWN WORDS

'My name is Angelikí Stávrou. I am 91 years old. I was 20 years old when my husband went to my father to ask for my hand in marriage. I worked on my father's farm then. My husband and I didn't know each other well but we fell in love at a distance. In those days young men and women didn't have many opportunities to mix with each other. When young girls went out, they were usually accompanied by their father or brother. Brothers played a very important role in their sisters' lives. Things are very different today. It would be wonderful to be young now and have the freedom of young people today.'

Women's roles

The lives and experiences of young Greek women today are very different from those of previous generations. Traditionally Greek girls were brought up to have a domestic role, remaining in the home to look after their husband and family and do the household tasks. If the family had land or animals, they were expected to help with agricultural work, too. Today's young women have the freedom to come and go from their homes, to dress as they like, and to socialise with friends, both male and female. They are encouraged to go to university, and to pursue careers and good jobs.

As the Greek way of life has shifted from one based on agriculture to one based on consumerism, it has become increasingly necessary for both parents in a family to go out to work if they wish to maintain a good standard of living. So, although Greek women today have greater independence, life has not necessarily become easier for them as they struggle to cope with the demands of a job, looking after the home and family, and a faster and more stressful pace of life.

▲ *Many young Greek women are fashion and fitness conscious.*

◄ *Women on motor scooters are a common sight in Greece's towns and cities.*

Changes in youth culture

One of the areas of swiftest change in recent decades is in the interests and pursuits of young people. Greek parents are far less strict with their teenagers than in the past, and are more likely to be supportive of their youngsters' individual interests, talents and career choices. Children and teenagers today also possess many more things of their own. Increasing exposure, due mainly to tourism and television, to the fashions, music and youth culture of Western Europe and America, means that young Greeks tend to listen to the same music, see the same films, watch the same or similar television programmes, and wear the same fashions as in other Western cultures.

▲ *Most households today possess a colour television and a video recorder.*

IN THEIR OWN WORDS

'I'm Victoria Giliánou. I'm 25 and I work in a photographic studio. I enjoy my work but when I get married and have children, I wouldn't want to work full-time. But part-time work is hard to find in Greece, and it usually is poorly paid. When I get married I will keep my name and add it to my husband's name. This is quite usual in Greece. The children don't take their mother's surname, only their father's.

'Women are no longer the servants of their husbands as they were in the past. We are educated enough now to have a role equal to that of men. There has to be a balance and now there is. Things will get better for women as they gain a greater say in the work place. I would like to give my daughters a good education. Hopefully, they will speak three foreign languages: English, French and German or Spanish.'

Religion

Nearly all Greeks are Greek Orthodox, a form of Christianity. There is a small minority of Catholics, most of whom are found on the Ionian and Aegean islands. Their Orthodoxy is central to most Greeks' sense of identity. Nevertheless, the last thirty years have seen a decline in church attendance and fewer people are following their religious beliefs. Fewer men are entering the priesthood despite the fact that a Greek priest can almost be guaranteed a secure income and social status within his community.

On the other hand, nearly every Greek person's life is affected by religious rituals and feast days, with Easter and the Assumption of the Virgin, on the 15th August, as the most important events of the religious calendar. In contrast to the commercial nature of Christmas in many countries, for example, Easter still has enormous spiritual significance to the Greeks. It is a time when Greek people return to their

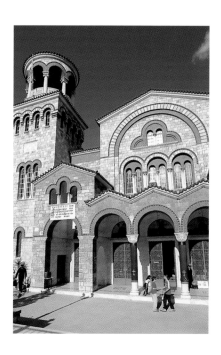

▲ *A modern Orthodox church built in the Byzantine style.*

IN THEIR OWN WORDS

'I'm Mákis Giannakópoulos. I'm 14 years old and I was born here in Athens. I go to church once or twice a month, usually because my friends or grandparents ask me to go with them. During Easter Holy Week I go every day. My family always go to the Good Friday evening service when we all follow the procession of the Epitáfios that symbolises Christ's funeral bier. Then on Saturday night we celebrate Christ's resurrection. It's a great occasion.

'Greece is becoming a less religious society. Young people and teenagers like me have other idols to care about. We're interested in pop stars and footballers. But Greek people are still superstitious. Nearly everybody believes in *to máti*, or the evil eye, whatever their background, wherever they live. Our families instil it into us as children. The evil eye is connected to envy. If somebody admires something about you, say a neighbour looks with admiration at a newborn child, or something special you've just bought, although they are intending you no harm, they may be casting the evil eye on you. You may feel poorly, perhaps feel sick or get a headache. Then you have to visit someone with the power to take the evil away from you.'

home village or town to join other family members in the local processions and rituals. Special Easter foods are cooked and the Lenten fast, during which meat and other animal foods should not be eaten, is still observed by many Greeks, including the young.

Foreign influences

Name days have always been more important than birthdays in Greece. Each church, village and town in Greece is associated with a particular saint, and most people are named after a saint. On their particular saint's day their namesakes are visited by friends and family who are offered a *kérasma*, or treat, of cakes and sweetmeats and, for the adults, sweet liqueurs. In recent decades, however, as a result of increased contact with other customs and traditions, more and more Greek children and young adults celebrate their birthdays.

▲ *A recreation of Jesus' funeral bier is decorated with flowers for the Good Friday Epitáfios procession.*

▼ *At the end of the Easter Saturday mass, everybody carries home a lighted candle.*

Education

Greeks have always placed a high value on education. Children are encouraged to work hard, right from their first school years. The state provides free education, from primary school through to university. The school day is shorter than in many European countries but, alongside a large amount of homework, most children have after-school lessons in foreign languages or perhaps music. Many attend private schools in the afternoons and evenings for extra tuition in their weaker subjects, especially if they are preparing for university entrance.

▲ *A group of children on their way home from school at midday.*

The education system has changed little in recent decades, the basic curriculum and teaching methods remain the same. The emphasis is still very much on learning facts rather than developing a critical mind and expressing ideas.

As in many countries, Greek education is facing problems, such as low pay for teachers and a lack of facilities. Few schools have libraries, science laboratories or computers. In urban schools, shortage of space is often a problem.

IN THEIR OWN WORDS

'My name is Faní Balamóti. I am a teacher in a *lykeio*, or High School, for 15- to 18-year-olds in Kalambáka, a town of some 12,000 people. The school has about 100 pupils in each year, which are divided into five groups. Altogether the students have an average of 35 teaching hours per week followed by 3-4 hours at a *frontistírio*, a private school, every day and at least 3 hours homework.

'Almost every Greek family dreams of a University degree for their children. If a student fails to get into a Greek university, many go abroad to finish their education. I feel that students and their families should realise that a university degree is no longer a guarantee for future employment and that they should be more open and flexible.'

Leisure and sport

Socialising with friends and family is the main leisure activity in Greece. This mainly takes place outside the home, in cafés and restaurants, especially during the summer when small city apartments become unbearably hot. Music is important to all generations of Greeks and is central to Greek culture. Much traditional Greek music, which combines eastern and western influences, is still played live at religious and cultural gatherings, as well as in tavernas and clubs. During the summer months, lots of Greeks enjoy open-air concerts, plays, dance productions and film shows.

The most popular spectator sports are football and basketball, which are followed with passion. Sporting activities are practised mainly by the younger generations. Athletics, jogging, volleyball, swimming, sailing and wind-surfing are all popular activities.

▲ *Busy trade in a café filled with young Athenians. Frappé, or cold coffee – drunk white or black – is a popular drink at all times of the day.*

▶ *City dwellers enjoy a cycle ride at a weekend.*

Diet and health

For thousands of years Greek cuisine has changed very little. The traditional diet consists of plenty of vegetables, salads and pulses. Meat and fish are eaten about twice a week. Bread is eaten at every meal. Recent decades, however, have seen new trends in people's eating habits. The main meal of the day used to be prepared and cooked in the morning and eaten at a late lunch. As Greek wives and mothers are now going out to work, they are no longer able to shop on a daily basis and have little time to prepare a large midday meal. Consequently there has been a trend not only towards eating the main meal in the evening, but also to eating convenience foods and take-away foods.

Traditional Greek takeaway foods are *souvlákia*, or kebabs, and cheese pies, but pizzas and hamburger bars are now found everywhere. Supermarkets have introduced people to many other 'non-Greek' foods. In the past children seldom ate breakfast other than a glass of warm milk, while now many homes have cereals in their cupboard.

▲ *The majority of Greeks buy their fresh fruit and vegetables from street markets and greengrocers.*

◄ *American style fast-food restaurants are common throughout Greece.*

IN THEIR OWN WORDS

'My name is Yiannis Koutendakis. I've always had an interest in food and I enjoy cooking now. I like cooking 'adventurous' food – like Spanish, Chinese and Indian dishes. Of course that's not typical of Greeks. Greek men today still don't do a lot of cooking apart from barbecues and light meals, like pasta.

'When I was growing up our diet varied from season to season. Now we can buy whatever we want all through the year. We avoid fast food, except for an occasional pizza. You see lots of children snacking on crisps and things. We offer our children fruit rather than crisps, though we do allow them chocolate, but almost never fizzy drinks! My family on Crete always supply us with olive oil. In fact I never remember buying olive oil. Most people have a contact with an oil producer so they buy direct from them. In that way, things aren't so different from the past.'

Health provision

Greece's National Health System was established in 1983 to provide state-funded care. People are entitled to free treatment from doctors, and pay only a small proportion of medication costs. Greece is well supplied with doctors and today there are health centres in most villages.

The traditional Mediterranean diet, based on fresh produce, olive oil rather than animal fats, and little meat, is regarded as one of the healthiest in the world. As Greeks have become wealthier, they have increased their consumption of meat and processed foods. This has brought new health problems such as obesity, heart disease and diabetes.

▼ *Despite public awareness of the health risks associated with cigarettes, Greeks are some of Europe's heaviest smokers.*

8

Changes at Work

Employment

Greece has traditionally been a country of small, family-run businesses. To be self-employed and to have one's own business is usually seen as preferable to working for other people. With the exception of certain professions and the civil service, being an employee was regarded as having little control over one's working life, with poor entitlement to holidays, sick leave, or pensions, as well as low wages. However, with rising industrialization and the emergence of large companies, employment conditions and job security prospects have improved. Today, of Greece's approximate 4.5 million employed people, some 60 per cent work in the service sector, and about 20 per cent each in industry and agriculture.

▼ *Small shops, such as this specialist cured meat shop, are often family businesses with no or few paid staff.*

Women at work

In the 1980s and 1990s, huge numbers of Greek women joined the salaried workforce. Women now make up over half the numbers employed in retailing and office jobs. Work in education, health care and other areas of the civil service are considered particularly appropriate for women. Women also make up over 50 per cent of the unskilled work force.

◄ *Athenian women shoppers in a pedestrian precinct. Athens has many chic and fashionable shopping districts.*

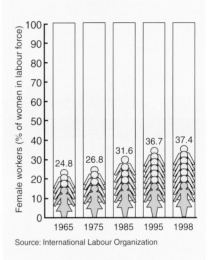

Female workers (% of women in labour force)

24.8 (1965) 26.8 (1975) 31.6 (1985) 36.7 (1995) 37.4 (1998)

Source: International Labour Organization

Despite the passing of laws regarding equality of the sexes women are still less likely to be in positions of management and responsibility. Women's salaries are often lower than those of their male colleagues. And when it comes to family businesses, they may not have an equal say in decision making.

▲ *The number of women in the workplace continues to grow as younger generations pursue careers and not the traditional domestic role.*

IN THEIR OWN WORDS

'My name is Ada Christophe. I run an English-language school. A lot of women in Greece are now doing jobs that were traditionally male jobs. You often see women driving buses and taxis. Women are forced to work now because life is so expensive. Few companies provide nurseries so there is a growing demand for child-minders. The state provides some pre-school care, and it's free, but there is a need for much more. My working hours are between 4 p.m. and 10 p.m. at night which doesn't make it easy for me, as I am a single-mother with a six-year-old son.'

Manufacturing

Compared to other EU countries, Greece's industrial activity remains low. Long-established manufacturing industries include petrochemicals, cement, cigarettes and textiles, including cotton goods and blankets. Greece no longer relies on imported domestic electrical appliances, for today it manufactures 'white goods' such as fridges and washing machines and other electrical goods. In recent years food processing has become a particularly successful growth industry, while tourism has massively boosted the market for soft drink industries. Most of the country's large industries are concentrated around Athens. Tourism has helped to sustain and generate new, light manufacturing industries (for example, pottery, woodwork and souvenir making) in areas other than the big cities.

Evolving industries

The last decade has seen the rapid rise of ownership of computers and mobile phones in all areas of Greek life. Today information technology, electronic commerce and telecommunications are among

▲ *The spread of tourism has brought about a huge increase in the number of people working in restaurants, bars and cafés.*

◄ *Mobile phones are both cheap to buy and use. Most Greek households now possess at least one mobile phone.*

IN THEIR OWN WORDS

'My name is Theódoros Papatheódorou. I'm 23 years old and I work as a computer programmer for a bank. My job involves writing software to assess people's credit risk. In my free time I like to take photographs with my digital camera.

'Most people have computers now. The internet is the main reason that Greeks use them. Lots of young people have email accounts, and nearly everyone has a mobile phone. Myself, I don't like mobile phones, I think they are a plague to the country. But I think mobile phone technology and the possibility of selling and buying online are the big things of the future. Most businesses have a website and online selling is growing. Greece is trying to become a centre for information technology, rather like Ireland.'

the fastest growing areas in the Greek economy, and many young Greeks are choosing to train and work in these fields.

Other evolving industries include wine-making. Greeks have been making wine for thousands of years but until very recently, the wine industry was dominated by a handful of large companies. Today small wine businesses producing quality wines are found in Macedonia, the Peloponnese and on some of the islands.

One of Greece's recent success stories is fish farms. These range from small businesses to large companies with several hundred employees. Helped by subsidies from the EU, the number and size of Greek fisheries has grown rapidly. With increasing exports of farmed sea bream and sea bass to Europe, fish farming is making an increasingly significant contribution to the country's economy.

▼ Greece's coastline with its countless bays and clean waters is ideally suited to fish farming.

41

Shipping

With the largest merchant fleet in the world, shipping is a major contributor to Greece's economy. Other than Piraeus, Greece's biggest ports are Thessaloníki, Patrás, Vólos and Heráklion. Until the end of the 1980s shipping was one of the largest employers within the private sector. At the turn of the century there was a fall in the number of Greek shipping companies due partly to increasing pressure on them to modernize and upgrade their vessels to meet international safety standards. However, the shipping sector is still expanding and Greek-owned ships still operate all over the world, though today their crews consist mainly of foreign workers.

▲ *Piraeus is Greece's biggest port, and is one of the largest in the Mediterranean.*

Changing patterns of work

The working day in Greece varies according to the kind of business. For many Greeks, it may begin at 8 a.m. or earlier,

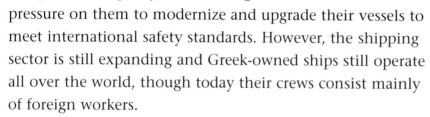

IN THEIR OWN WORDS

'My name is Kóstas Epaminóndas. I'm from Limassol, on Cyprus, but now I live in Athens. I started a business selling cars here in 1993. Originally I sold BMWs but now I specialise in Renaults. European cars sell well in Greece. There is no car manufacturing industry in the country and no cars are assembled here. All new cars have to be imported. About 250,000 new cars are bought every year. Despite the import duty, cars are cheaper in Greece than in many European countries. Petrol is cheap too. Most Greek families own at least one car. About ten years ago the Government brought in tax concessions for people who traded in an old car for a new car. New cars are less harmful to the environment and Athens has terrible pollution problems.'

and end between 1.30 p.m. or 3 p.m. For others,
(for example, the retail trade), the working day may fall into
two halves, with a long break for the afternoon siesta hours.
In the cities this results in four, rather than two, rush hours,
which contributes to pollution and congestion problems.

In the past the farming year dictated times of work and
rest. For many Greeks now, it is the tourist season that
determines this. In tourist areas, people regularly work for
17 or more hours a day, seven days a week during the tourist
season, as their shops, cafés or offices stay open all day and
late into the night. They then close their businesses between
late October and the following spring. During these months,
many people resume life in Athens or return to their villages
to tend to their land and crops, or simply to recover from the
long and hectic summer months.

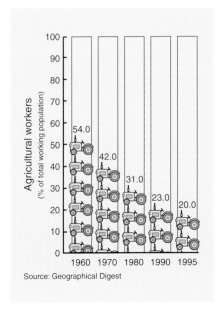

Source: Geographical Digest

▲ This graph shows Greece's
strong reliance on agriculture
in the past. This figure has
more than halved over the
last 30 years.

◄ Evening shoppers in Athens.
In summer shops remain open
until 8.30 p.m.

9

The Way Ahead

Greece lies at the crossroads between the East and the West. As a member of the EU, Greece is linked politically and economically with other member EU countries. Yet geographically, Greece is much closer to the other countries of south-east Europe. Political and economic events in the Balkans have had, and may continue to have, an enormous impact on Greece. During the 1990s, war and political turmoil in the former Yugoslavia and Albania meant that the main land route into Greece from Europe was cut-off for many years. It also brought about mass immigration from that area. On the other hand, the collapse of Communism in south-eastern Europe has led to the strengthening of Greece's trade links with its Balkan neighbours, including Turkey, although the two countries continue to have an uneasy relationship as a result of

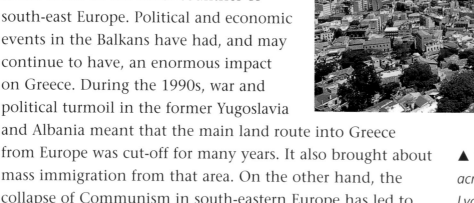

▲ The view from the Acropolis across Athens to Mount Lycabettus, the highest of the city's hills. The Greek national flag flies in the foreground.

IN THEIR OWN WORDS

'My name is Vangelis Thanos. My parents moved from the country to Athens, which they thought of as 'the promised land', hoping to find a good job and an easier and more comfortable life. I am a percussionist with an orchestra. Europe has a great influence on the Greek people. We try hard to be like other Europeans, but we are beginning to lose our sense of community and environment. And people don't care enough about things like pollution and the environment. They are more concerned with the present. I try to have a longer term attitude to life. The government and the media must make the environment a priority. There's too much political corruption in Greece. This has to change if we are to succeed as a country in the future. We have to change now if Greece in the future is to play a part in Europe and the world.'

historical issues and the unresolved problem of Turkish-occupied Cyprus.

In the last fifty years Greece has transformed from a traditional, non-industrial, agricultural society into a modern, prosperous consumer-orientated society. At the turn of the century, the rate of economic growth was faster than the average rate of that in other countries of the EU. Living standards have risen rapidly to a level above that enjoyed elsewhere in the Balkans. Great technological changes have taken place in a very short time. There have been vast improvements to the country's infrastructure, since the 2004 Olympic Games, which were held in Athens. The problems confronting Greece today are similar to those faced by countries elsewhere, such as crises in education and health, environmental issues, rising unemployment and immigration. Although there is a drug problem in the larger cities, overall there is relatively little poverty and crime, while family and community support is still strong. There is considerable optimism about the future, especially amongst the young.

▼ *The youth of Greece today has prospects that their grandparents could never have anticipated.*

Glossary

Acid rain Rain produced when sulphur dioxide and nitrogen oxides (gases released when fuels are burnt) dissolve into rainwater to fall as sulphuric or nitric acid.

Agriculture Farming the land to produce food.

Archipelago A sea with groups of many islands.

Bier The stand on which a coffin is placed and carried.

Birth rate The number of people born in a given area over a period of time.

Boreholes Wells dug deep into the earth to find water.

Caique A large, wooden fishing boat.

Cistern A tank for storing water.

Communists Followers of Communism believe that all people are equal and that all property should be publicly, as opposed to privately, owned.

Consumer society A society that is based on the purchase and consumption of goods and services.

Coup d'état Unlawful seizure of state power.

Culture The beliefs, customs, language and behaviour shared by a group of people.

Democracy A system of government in which the population vote for the person or party who will govern them.

Diaspora (Greek) The spread of a particular people throughout the world.

Domestic Literally meaning of the home, but also used to refer to national rather than international.

Economy All the business activity in a country.

European Union The association of European countries that have joined together to cooperate on matters relating to trade, taxation, agriculture, the environment, etc.

Fertilizers Chemicals and other substances used to add nutrients to the soil.

Hydro-electricity Electricity that is generated by the use of water to turn turbines.

Immigration Coming to live in a country from abroad.

Import To buy goods from other countries.

Income The money that people receive for their work or from their investments.

Junta The group of people, often from the army, who take power in a *coup d'état*.

Manufacturing The making of goods.

Monarchy The system of government that is led by a king or queen.

Mountain scrub Brushwood and wild, shrub-like vegetation that grows wild on a mountain.

NATO North Atlantic Treaty Organization.

Nomadic A wandering way of life, often determined by the seasons and location of pasture land for animals.

Package holidays A holiday with travel, accommodation and other arrangements included in the price.

Peninsula A piece of land that juts out into the sea.

Pesticides Chemicals used to destroy garden and crop pests.

Population The total number of people in a place at a given time.

Raptors Birds of prey.

Rural Relating to the countryside.

Subsidies Government money that is given to a particular group to help with a specific project.

Subsistence farming Farming to produce food to support the farmer and his family as opposed to farming to produce crops for sale.

Urban An urban area is built-up, such as a town or a city.

Further Information

Books to read
Focus on Greece by Brian Dicks (Evans
Brothers Ltd, 1992)
A Visit to Greece by Peter Roop (Heinemann
Library, 2000)
History of Emigration from Greece by Sofka
Zinovieff (Franklin Watts, 1997)

Useful addresses
Greek National Tourism Organization
4 Conduit Street,
London W1R ODJ
Tel : 020 7734 5997
Fax : 020 7287 1369
E-mail: greektouristoffice@btinternet.com

Greek Embassy
1A Holland Park
London W11 3TP
Tel.: 020 7221 0093 / 7221 5977
Fax: 020 7243 4212

Index

Numbers in **bold** are pages
where there is a photograph
or illustration.